Satan's Henchman

*What Ever Became of
SS General Hans Kammler?*

Robert Huddleston

Contents

Preface

BY MID-1943 IT WAS APPARENT ON BOTH sides of the European conflict that it was the beginning of the end of Germany's Third Reich. But when would Germany's "unconditional surrender" come? Each day of conflict produced thousands of new victims—women, children, the elderly—from Allied bombing of German population centers. Additional victims were the thousands of slave laborers being starved, beaten, tortured, and literally worked to death as Nazis demanded increased production of German weaponry.

Desperate, Hitler designated a little known SS general to be in charge of the entire German armaments industry, thus making him the third most powerful Nazi leader, no. 1 being Adolf Hitler and no. 2 the SS leader Heinrich Himmler.

Nazi leaders were determined to increase production of advanced military assets such as the Messerschmitt 262 (Me 262), a twin-engine jet fighter "capable of driving Allied bombers from the skies," boasted Luftwaffe leader Hermann Göring; the V-1, a jet-propelled bomb; and most importantly, the V-2 ballistic rocket with a 200-plus-mile range that included London and other British cities. "Maximize production whatever the cost," ordered Hitler, dooming thousands of slave laborers to being worked to death.

SS General Hans Kammler took on his assigned responsibilities with intense zeal. Soon, however, he realized that Hitler demanded the impossible. Wisely, he decided to distance himself from his leader by relocating his headquarters from Berlin to Munich. Shortly thereafter, he arrived in his private train in the city of Nordhausen, home of the underground factory producing the V-2 rocket.

Knowing he would be targeted as a war criminal, Kammler decided to negotiate his freedom. He rounded up hundreds of German rocket experts, packed them into his private railway train, and headed to German-held territory in Bavaria. His goal was to insure his freedom from Allied justice, along with a ticket to South America in exchange for the rocket experts that the Allies coveted. His planned proposition to the Allies:

"If there's no deal, they die. Your choice!"

Before contact could be made with the American forces, however, Hitler caught up with Kammler and ordered him to proceed to Prague to take command of an SS division defending the city from Soviet forces. From there, the general disappeared, his fate becoming a contentious issue and spurring much speculation.

And that, dear reader, is what the tale of *Satan's Henchman* is all about. It is a recounting of one of the most powerful and sinister among the evil lot that led Germany's Third Reich to ultimate defeat. It is a biography that requires some imagination to complete the story and in the process becomes a historical novel.

1

A Strange Death
in the West

From the unpublished notes of Bert Wellborn

THE LAST TIME I SAW THIS CHARACTER he was on the way to a hanging—his own. So what the hell was he doing in the El Rancho Hotel in Gallup, New Mexico, in September 1951? But then, what was as I doing in Gallup, New Mexico?

I'm a newspaper reporter between jobs, having left the *Globe-Democrat* in St. Louis headed to the *Times* in Los Angeles, where I'd been offered the role of political reporter covering the 1952 presidential election. This came about through a World War II connection related to this tale. I had gotten banged-up in the Battle of the Bulge, not bad enough to be sent home but enough to get duty less arduous than toting an M1 rifle and digging foxholes. The officer doing the assigning noted I had been on my high school newspaper and decided the army's *Stars and Stripes* newspaper could keep me occupied until I was fit to return to the infantry. Fortunately, the war in Europe ended sooner than my recovery.

My wartime stint as a reporter led me to take advantage of the GI Bill at the University of Missouri. With a degree in journalism, bolstered by my experience on the *Stars and Stripes*, the St. Louis *Globe-Democrat* took me on as a cub reporter. After a year of learning the craft, I was assigned the political beat at city hall with occasional side trips to the state capital in Jefferson City. All was going well until I began to notice how the very conservative *Globe-Democrat* was editing my copy with a distinct shift to the right. My first complaint brought a "just your imagination" from the editor. If so, my imagination was in high gear as we approached the 1952 political season. Got to move on before I inherit a reputation I don't deserve, was my solution.

Some months earlier I had encountered my former *Stars and Stripes* editor in the St. Louis rail terminal. A spell in the bar of rehashing the war ended with his words, "Let's keep in touch." Since he was now an editor at the *Los Angeles Times*, I decided it was time to get in touch. I called, he needed a political reporter, and I headed west. I was also stimulated, I might add, by a painful failed love affair.

St. Louis to Los Angeles meant traveling historic US 66. In Gallup it became Main Street, the place where my 1942 Ford malfunctioned. I was directed to Dave's Garage. "No big problem," was Dave's assessment. "Only I've got to get you a new part out of Albuquerque and that means tomorrow at the earliest. If they have it, it will be on the next Greyhound bus." We talked a bit and discovered we had both been young GIs rushed into the Battle of the Bulge with little training against Germany's vaunted SS Panzers. Now we were buddies, especially when I mentioned my Purple Heart and stint on the *Stars and Stripes*.

"Great newspaper," he said. "That was the only way we knew what the hell was going on. And Bill Mauldin was as good as they get. Hope he's still alive."

"He is," I responded, in reference to the political cartoonist, "and giving the politicians as much hell as he gave the brass." I nodded to the wall. "I see by your license you're David Radosovich. Meet Bert Wellborn," I said as I offered my hand. "Now, tell me, how did a Slav land among the Indians?"

Laughing Dave said, "Granddaddy came west in the late 1800s to work the coal mines. Gallup started as a coal stop for the railroad. Lots of coal. Made some people a lot of money, but little for the miners."

"Then came diesel," I contributed. "What keeps Gallup going now?"

"New mines, uranium. Tourists. Indians—Navaho, Zuni, some Hopis—come here to shop and sell jewelry, blankets, and pottery, especially when the Santa Fe Chief and Superchief come through. It's a fast stop, but the passengers buy like hell before jumping back aboard."

"So I've got a night among the Indians, maybe two. What do I do to keep out of trouble?"

"First you sign in at Motel 66 on the next street. You can get a nice clean room for less than five dollars. Then head out to the El Rancho Hotel—an easy walk. Have a beer only, too pricey to eat. A nice plate of enchiladas and fried beans at the rail station will run less than a buck. Just happens my brother, George, is the barkeep at the El Rancho, and I'll alert him you're on the way. It's the show place of Gallup, and you'll enjoy it. They film a lot of movies around here, and you might run into John Wayne. Better yet, Lana Turner."

The El Rancho was impressive. Coming into the lobby, hanging from a high balcony, was an immense Indian blanket—could be the largest ever made. "The Indian Capital of the World," as Gallup advertised itself, was reflected in the Indian artifacts that lined the lobby and carried over into the bar and lounge area.

I introduced myself, "Bert Wellborn from St. Louis."

George greeted me like a long-lost customer. The beer was cold and costly but just what I needed. George, it turned out, was also a vet from the European war.

Between beers I made a trip to the men's room and barely settled back on my bar stool when I glanced at two men entering the bar. The tallest of the two sent a shock down my spine.

"George, those two," I nodded, "know them?"

"Not local," offered George without looking up from mixing a martini. "The big guy's up from

Las Cruces, said to be one of the German rocket types at the army's testing base. The guy with a limp has been around about a week, so quiet he's hardly left a shadow. Rumored to have been buying up uranium claims east of here around Grants. Probably to turn them over to make a quick profit. Gimpy Leg is an alien asshole. Demanded an offbeat German beer I didn't have, then bitched. Up his."

When they sat at the bar and began speaking German, I gave them my meanest look and said, "Gentlemen, speaking German during the war attracted the FBI. Now, as one who fought in that bloody war, it upsets me to hear German. Do you mind?"

They just stared back at me, the gimpy guy with a look as mean as mine. They huddled together and began conversing in broken English. I stayed close and heard a couple of things, about a bank account and the ugly asshole bragging about building barracks.

Gimpy Leg was a stranger to me, but it was the other guy I knew as a real asshole. I knew him as a war criminal certain to meet a date with the hangman. Rudolf Baumann. The one and only time we had met was at the tail-end of the war near the German city of Nordhausen. *Stars and Stripes* had received a call from a tank commander saying they had liberated one of the worst Nazi concentration camps and wanted it covered. I was available, and off I went. What I found and wrote is on the front page of the *Stars and Stripes'* April 1945 edition: "Tunnels of Hell: 22,000 Nazi Slaves Made V-2s in Deep Underground Factory." Later, *Life* featured photographs of the dead prisoners "stacked like cordwood." The dead and living slaves represented all nations conquered by the Nazis. Labor was cheap and expendable.

American war crimes investigators estimated that from late 1943 until captured in April 1945, as many as 70,000 slave laborers worked in the vast underground factory. An estimated 22,000 died of disease, starvation, beatings, and executions while forced to produce Hitler's "revenge weapon," the V-2 rocket, and other advanced weaponry. When I arrived, hundreds of emaciated bodies, still unburied, were laid out in rows. Baumann had been captured in a nearby village claiming to be a retired university professor with no connection to the underground factory. Several surviving prisoners, however, identified him as the production manager who authorized and witnessed the many hangings of prisoners for acts such as accidentally dropping a rocket part. While I was recording the terrible scene, Baumann came escorted by a US Army major and two military police. "Haughty" was how I described him in my report. The army major, a war crimes investigator named Ben Wilder, said they had a hard time keeping Baumann from being lynched by surviving prisoners but wanted him in good shape for the trial and hanging.

Rudolf Baumann being in New Mexico in September 1951, six years following his capture at Nordhausen, was a story that had to be told. How had he been able to avoid prosecution as a war criminal, and who had been instrumental in helping him escape that fate? My insight into politics told me that the "fix" had to be high up in the US government since the army had him in custody in 1945. A call to my future boss at the *L.A. Times* generated much interest but convinced me that it was an investigation that had to wait until after the next election.

I was stuck in Gallup an extra day waiting for the needed part to get my '42 Ford running, so managed a bit of sightseeing in and around

Gallup. Early the second morning, I had a call from my new-found friend George the barkeep.

"Thought you'd like to know, your Nazi guy, Baumann, turned up dead yesterday. According to my buddy in the sheriff's office, he was out on a mine site with the other guy, and he slipped and fell off a cliff ..."

"No shit."

"The guy with the gimpy leg is Herman White, said to be from New Jersey. Seems he gave a statement to the sheriff about trying to keep Baumann from the edge but the asshole went anyway, slipped and fell about fifty feet. Rocks below did him in. That satisfied the coroner and the death was considered an accident."

Too easy on the bastard, I thought. Not a charitable feeling on my part, but the vision—and smell—of those dead slaves had never gone away.

2
He Was an Ugly Guy
with a Limp ...

*Continuing from the unpublished
notes of Bert Wellborn*

WHEN I REACHED THE OFFICE OF THE *Santa Fe New Mexican*, I found Hillerman waiting. He led me to a nearby cafe and ordered two beers. George had alerted me as to what to expect: a tall, lanky, sun-baked ex-farm boy with ears more like wing flaps. "But don't underestimate the smarts inside that rough and tough exterior," George warned. "He's one sharp ex-GI who came home with two Silver Stars and a Purple Heart." Hillerman and I replayed the European conflict and agreed the brass had screwed up the Battle of the Bulge. "Had they listened to the GIs on the front, they would have known the Krauts were gathering for an offensive attack," declared Hillerman. Brass hubris, we two journalists concluded.

After exchanging how we got into journalism—first college under the GI Bill, then going wherever a door opened to practice the craft—I described my experience at the *Globe Democrat*. Hillerman shared his experience reporting for small newspapers, "You learn a lot, good and bad about people," before being assigned to Santa Fe by the UPI, then to the *Santa Fe New Mexican* as a general reporter.

When we came 'round to why we were meeting, we both agreed that if an officially recognized Nazi war criminal became an honored American citizen, higher officials had to be involved. That, as any reporter would know, was a lead story.

I was pleased that Hillerman had read the April 17, 1945, issue of the *Stars and Stripes*, a copy having been supplied by George. He especially appreciated "Tunnels of Hell" appearing in my article's headline. He commented—with a smile—that it was interesting that the Germans had an automated rocket production line, no managers required. Learning who the leaders were was easy, he pointed out. You simple informed a captured SS guard that it was a question of being turned over to the Russians or becoming a POW of the British or Americans. On that basis I learned that SS General Hans Kammler, whom none appeared to know, was in charge of the entire rocket complex, with the now-deceased German civilian Rudolf Baumann in charge of production. With Baumann having been eliminated, full attention could be devoted to bringing the SS general to an accounting. I included the two, Kammler and Baumann, in my copy, but their names were excluded in the editing. It was as if the editor or the publisher sensed that a conflict lay ahead with the Soviet Union and that Germany would be on our side. There it was: our enemy's enemy was our friend.

The *Stars and Stripes* feature stimulated the *Santa Fe New Mexican* reporter to arrange a visit to the White Sands Missile Range, where he was able to interview Major James "Jim" Harper, the US Army officer responsible for Nazi party member Wernher von Braun and upwards of one hundred of von Braun's rocket experts (selected by him) being brought to the US and being employed as army civil servants. It was America's future space-age hero who selected Rudolf Baumann to be employed by the US government. No way to untie those two, so Dr. von Braun's Nazi membership and commission in the SS was expunged from the record, and Baumann's Nazi past apparently followed.

I informed Hillerman that I had been in contact with the war crimes investigator Major Ben Wilder. Wilder had stayed behind after I departed the Nazi rocket complex but later returned for the trial of the few suspects that had been apprehended, the leading suspects having faded into the German civil communities. Wernher von Braun and his most recent boss, SS Obergruppenführer [Lieutenant General] Hans Kammler, were among those who eluded being apprehended.

I recounted that journalists, as well as most officials, were confused about the German organization for V-2 development and production in an underground factory. Major Wilder had drawn a flowchart to aid me in understanding the operation.

Production in the underground factory was provided by the Mittelwerk company under a contract with the SS. The required [slave] labor was procured and provided by the SS, mostly from the Buchenwald concentration camp some forty miles distant. Until the fall of 1944, the prisoners—many from France—were delivered directly to the underground factory where they were housed and worked on a 24-7 schedule. Pressed by the V-2 production manager, who was held to a production quota, the SS finally constructed Dora, a concentration camp adjacent to the underground facility where prisoners were starved and beaten at the will of the SS and guards, mostly German criminals called Kapos. When no longer able to work, prisoners were cremated or dumped into the Boelcke-Kaserne, a former German army barrack located in the city of Nordhausen. These were the thousands of dead and dying workers discover by the American Third Armored Division when they occupied the city on April 11, 1945, and provided the details for the April 17 *Stars and Stripes* front-page news report. Prisoners still able to work had been moved north to be reincarcerated in the Belsen concentration camp. Some managed to complete the journey by rail or foot, others were slaughtered or fell to advancing Allied forces.

(The extermination of a thousand people in a barn set on fire was later revealed by an American unit that captured the town of Gardenlagen.)

In mid-1944, Reichfürher Heinrich Himmler, head of the SS, had gained control of the V-2 missile complex and placed SS General Hans Kammler in charge. What follows is a detailed description of the general and his appointment by Hitler to direct the German rocket and jet aircraft programs under the immediate supervision of Himmler:

Hans Frederik Karl Kammler was born in Stettin, Germany, on August 28, 1901. Disappointed at being too young to serve in the Great War of 1914-1918, Kammler volunteered for military service in 1919 and completed his education in architecture, receiving his doctorate of architecture in November 1932. He had joined the Nazi party in 1931, and his architecture background and experience in construction led to advancement in rank and importance of assigned projects. He supported Adolf Hitler, not as an opportunist, but as a true believer in the Nazi ideology, extermination of the Jews, an aggressive military to expand Germany's borders in the east, and the use of slave labor whenever necessary.

True to the Nazi faith, Hans Kammler received his most (in)famous assignment in the spring of 1940, the design and construction of the Auschwitz concentration camp. Kammler added a personal feature, gas and cremation facilities that were capable of more efficient and effective mass murder.

Rocket production ended in March 1945 with upwards of six thousand produced, many of which clobbered London and other cities, though these bombings did not change the ultimate outcome of the war. The officially designated "A4" rocket had become the "V-2," the V for vergeltungswalle (translated as reprisal weapon). At this stage of the war, the V-2 attacks were not only in response to the Allied bombing campaign of enemy population centers, but also because the British continued to oppose Germany, forcing Hitler to fight on two fronts when his main target was the Soviet Union.

Early in 1945, General Kammler had drawn up a list of the leading rocket experts, and on April 2, 1945, hundreds of technicians, scientists, and engineers, under the "protection" of a hundred of Kammler's SS guards, embarked on a special train loaded with food and drink for an unannounced destination, later discovered to be the Bavarian Alps. On April 3 and 4, shortly following Kammler's departure, Nordhausen, shorn of military targets, was bombed by the Allies. Three quarters of the city was destroyed, with more than eight thousand dead civilians. It was an open secret that Allied intelligence had identified a number of high-ranking Nazis to be assassinated. Kammler had made the list but had escaped the bombing attempt. Though soon billeted in comfortable quarters near Oberammergau in southern Germany, the "rocketeers" accepted that they were prisoners and pawns to be exchanged for

> *a one-way ticket to a safe haven for Gen-*
> *eral Kammler, a reality confirmed later*
> *by Wernher von Braun.*

After Hillerman and Major Jim Harper had gotten to know one another through their European combat connection, Harper opened up about his distaste for the Germans. His assigned duty was to get them to an army base in El Paso, Texas, not to become their "host." He did, however, acknowledge that during their rail trip from New York to El Paso, von Braun opened up about SS General Kammler.

The mere mention of General Kammler, Harper recalled, generated a tone of hatred and foreboding from von Braun. Hitler and Himmler spawned killing, but Kammler, according to many prisoners, was an inhumane monster blind to the suffering of his prisoners.

America's future space-age hero Dr. Wernher von Braun began the long rail journey with Major Harper by giving a rambling and obviously self-serving account of the German rocket program. He had an excellent arrangement, he bragged, with the German army and General

Dornberger, his initial superior, dating back to the early 1930s. The Führer had no interest in rockets until after the landings at Normandy. After that point, he convinced himself that rocket attacks on London would lead to Britain withdrawing from the conflict. Once Hitler became interested, Himmler moved in to take over the program with General Kammler in charge, first to prepare the underground factory at Nordhausen, later to produce V-1s, V-2s, and advanced aircraft such as the Me 262 jet fighter, all at the cost of thousands of dead and dying forced-laborers. Von Braun confirmed that Kammler had taken him, along with hundreds of rocket workers, under SS guards to an army facility near Oberammergau in the Bavarian Alps. All this was known to Major Harper. While they were domiciled in comfortable barracks, von Braun emphasized that they were under house arrest and monitored by SS guards. "We were pawns," von Braun declared several times to Major Harper. In exchange for a new identity and safe haven, Kammler would deliver von Braun and the entire German rocket and advanced aircraft experts. This was related to von Braun by Kammler's deputy, who remained in charge following Kammler's departure. The SS officer also stated that should Kammler be killed, the rocket experts would be executed to keep them from capture by the Allies, especially the Soviet Union. Fortunately for von Braun, Kammler's deputy did not feel that murdering the lead rocket expert and his flock was in his best interest and he soon disappeared.

After von Braun's and Major Harper's train departed Kansas City, on the last leg of the journey to El Paso, Texas, von Braun completed his account of his connection to SS General Hans Kammler. The horrible treatment of workers, von Braun insisted, fell on the shoulders of Kammler and the SS, not on the German rocket experts.

After a few days at Oberammergau, a young SS officer appeared and was seen to present a document to Kammler, after which the SS general departed and "was never seen again." It was later accepted—but not confirmed—that he had proceeded to Prague, taken command of an SS division opposing Soviet forces, and had been killed in the fighting on May 9, 1945, one day after Germany's unconditional surrender. If so, it was too easy an end for Satan's Henchman, the label pinned on him in recognition of his overweening arrogance and ruthlessness, as evidenced by the deaths averaging 160 every day in the Tunnels of Hell.

(This is the end of Bert Wellborn's unpublished notes.)

3
The Tunnels of Hell

Following the exploits of Ben Wilder

THE DEATH OF GERMAN-AMERICAN Rudolf Baumann remained an "accident" in official police records in New Mexico. The two journalists, Wellborn and Hillerman, knew otherwise but chose not to pursue the matter. Hillerman was one white man that the Navahos respected. And Hillerman had learned that a young Navaho had witnessed the guy with the gimpy leg push the other guy, Baumann, off the cliff. Did the witness report this to the sheriff? No way! Navahos and the white authorities existed in different worlds. At the time of the incident, the young Navaho was hiding in the rocks consuming a jug of Gallo red, a violation of the white man's law. Absent sworn testimony from this unknown young Navaho, there was no basis for a criminal investigation. In this case the unspoken opinion was that justice had prevailed.

Thus ends the involvement of two journalists in the death of the German-American rocket expert Rudolf Baumann. Bert Wellborn returned to the *L.A. Times* as a political reporter. In due course, however, he returned to his former hometown, St. Louis, to woo and wed his college sweetheart and then relocated to the nation's capital as a *Washington Post* reporter, an assignment that led to a Pulitzer prize for his coverage of Richard Nixon's rise and fall.

Hillerman abandoned journalism to become an acclaimed novelist; his plots centered on the life and culture of America's southwest Indians of which he had become a recognized expert.

The war crimes unit, however, retained an intense interest in the life and death of Rudolf Baumann and the part he played in serving Adolf Hitler. Major Ben Wilder had been the principle source for Bert Wellborn's report on the underground V-2 factory published in the US Army's *Stars and Stripes* newspaper. The underground factory had been captured by American forces on April 11, and Wilder was there to apprehend and detain all possible war criminals as ordered by the Allied Supreme Commander General Eisenhower. Absent, however, were needed resources and active participation by the US military, who showed more interested in German military assets than in German war criminals.

Even before the conflict ended on May 8, 1945, Allied leaders had decided to divide a defeated Germany into zones controlled by the Allies. They also decided that German advanced military assets—including German experts such as von Braun and his rocket team, their research and production documents, and existing rockets—that were found in each zone would be shared with the other Allied countries, an agreement made with tongue in cheek. Even within the American military, each service vied to find and exploit advanced enemy assets.

In serving as a war crimes investigator, and subsequently as a prosecutor, it is noteworthy that Ben Wilder was the son of German-Jewish parents. Ben was born in Omaha, Nebraska, in 1914, a year after Neva and Leonard Wilder immigrated to America. Ben's dad, a master tailor, had been persuaded to come to Omaha to join a cousin in his highly successful tailoring business.

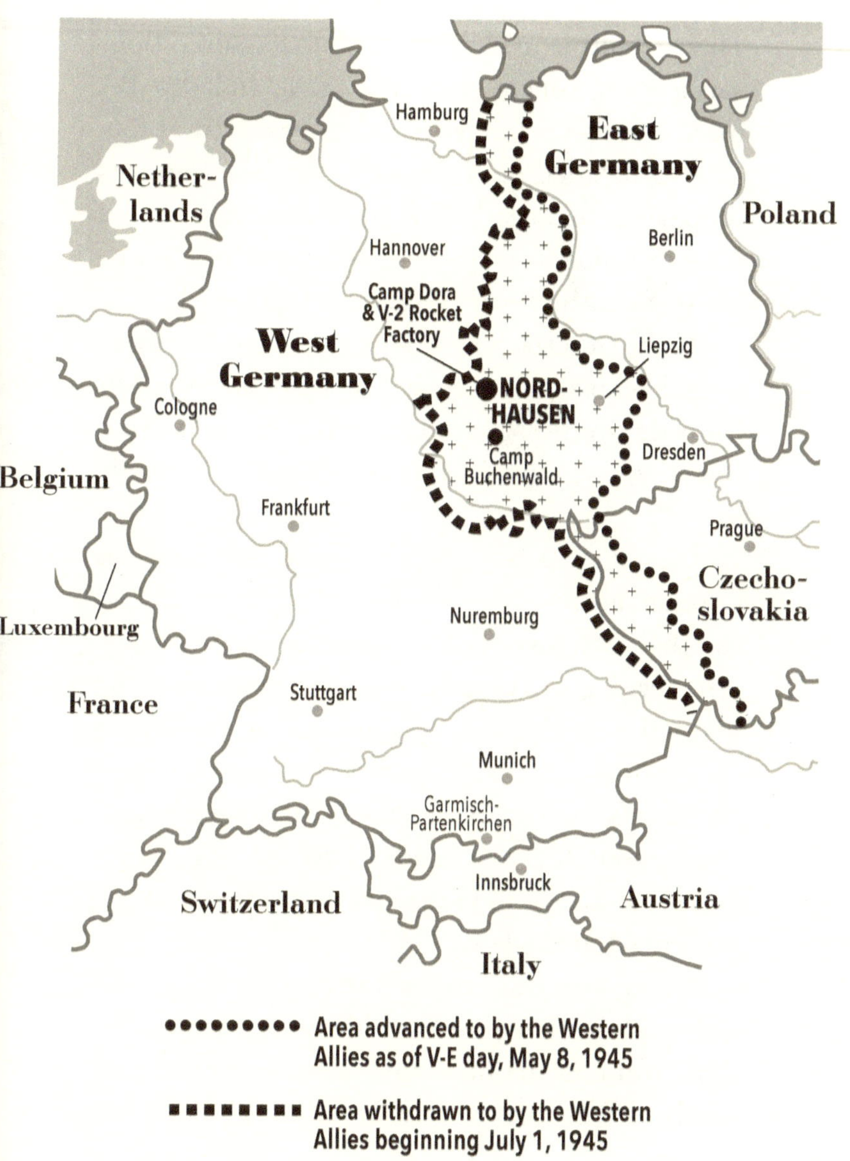
Netherlands
Hamburg
East Germany
Poland
Hannover
Berlin
Camp Dora & V-2 Rocket Factory
West Germany
Liepzig
Cologne
NORD-HAUSEN
Belgium
Camp Buchenwald
Dresden
Frankfurt
Prague
Luxembourg
Czecho-slovakia
France
Nuremburg
Stuttgart
Munich
Garmisch-Partenkirchen
Innsbruck
Switzerland
Austria
Italy
Area advanced to by the Western Allies as of V-E day, May 8, 1945
Area withdrawn to by the Western Allies beginning July 1, 1945

Their resulting middle-class status assured their son a good education, one that included a BA from Omaha's Creighton University in 1936. Having decided on a career in the law, Ben was preparing to enroll in Creighton's law school when a friend—as a joke—challenged him to apply to Yale, the country's no. 1 law school.

To his amazement, Ben was accepted—perhaps because they wanted at least one student from the midwest, he reasoned. This hick from the sticks was awarded a law degree cum laude in 1939.

Passed over by several private law firms in Omaha, attorney Ben Wilder became employed by the US Justice Department in Washington, serving in the criminal division. Following his first year, he was approached by the Office of Strategic Services (OSS), the federal government's newly established intelligence and counter-intelligence agency eager to employ an American fluent in German and trained and experienced in the law.

Upon entering the service, the OSS official explained, Wilder would receive basic military training at the army's Camp Richie, just north of Washington in Maryland. As far as his fellow students knew, he was just another Jewish-American with knowledge of and fluent in German. But following his army training, he would become an OSS agent with the rank of captain. (Off the record, the OSS official said the director, a major general, didn't care one whit about military status or rank. The OSS had military doing civilian jobs and civilians performing military ones. The philosophy was that it was what one can do, not who who one was that counted.)

As an agent of the OSS, most of Captain Wilder's involvement in the war consisted of interviewing captured Germans as part of a special program. Boring, yes, but illuminating to one eager to understand the Nazis and their war crimes. Early on, no interrogated German admitted any knowledge of a Nazi official named Hans Kammler. However, in early 1943 it became known that Kammler was the designer and builder of the Auschwitz concentration camp, an enterprise required to employ slave labor. He steadily advanced within the Nazi party that he had joined back in 1931 He also had enlisted in the SS at the time it was organized. With the completion of Auschwitz came advancement and recognition within the Nazi and SS leadership, but it also established his status as a war criminal.

As the war entered its final year before Germany's ultimate defeat, Kammler became the third most powerful leader in the Third Reich; Hitler and Himmler ranked one and two.

In April 1945, when Ben Wilder was attached to a unit that followed the combat forces into Nordhausen, US forces were focused on seizing German assets. These seizures were initially viewed as exploitation, but soon were referred to as "utilization," a more benign label. In July 1944, Supreme Headquarters of the Allied Expeditionary Force created units called T-Forces. These highly mobile, self-contained military units wore a large red "T" on their helmets and possessed the authority to seize and secure German military assets and to capture and hold alleged Nazi war criminals. This latter responsibility was virtually ignored in favor of exploiting Germany's military assets, included card-carrying Nazis and members of the SS.

Even before the conflict ended, it was apparent that the American military had little appetite for prosecuting German war criminals, except for the top Nazi leaders well-known to the American public. Had SS General Kammler been captured, he most certainly would have joined other Nazis in the dock at Nuremberg. In Kammler's absence, the British proposed that General Walter Dornberger, head of the German army's ballistic rocket program, take Kammler's place as retribution for the V-2 bombings of London. The Americans, however, were strongly opposed, perhaps realizing that prosecuting Dornberger would implicate von Braun, their prize German asset. It would be years before the public learned that Dr. von Braun had been a card-carrying Nazis, a commissioned member of the notorious SS, and had personally been involved in the use and abuse of slave labor for V-1 flying bombs, V-2 ballistic rockets, and jet fighter production. No doubt, the US military considered Germany a necessary ally in the almost certain hot or cold war against its World War II ally the Soviet Union.

The European Allied Command, recognizing that war crimes trials were in the future, established the War Crimes Unit under the US Army's judge advocate general in February 1945. Captain Ben Wilder immediately requested a transfer to the new organization. You will be considered, was the official response

Trials of alleged war criminals were not authorized to begin until June 19, 1945. This date would come and pass as differences surfaced between military units. Finally, Wilder, now a major, learned that all trials of alleged Nazi war criminals (those being tried at Nuremberg excepted) were to be conducted at the Dachau Concentration Camp to begin in November 1945.

The prosecution of war criminals was downplayed by America's military leaders; their principle goal was to locate and exploit advanced German military assets, especially those superior to Allied equipment. Examples included the German Tiger, the war's most outstanding heavy tank; the 88mm canon, excellent as field artillery, anti-tank weaponry, and as an anti-aircraft defense weapon; the Me 262, a twin-engined jet fighter far superior to the Allies' prop-driven fighters; and, of course, the Germans' long-range ballistic rockets, which the Allies had not developed during the war.

When it came to exploiting Nazi advanced technology, US Army Ordnance led the covetous pack with its Special Mission V-2, perhaps in acceptance of their past ignorance of the importance of ballistic rockets in strategic warfare. Operating out of Paris, the officer in charge of the mission, upon learning of the Nordhausen rocket complex, ordered the area guarded by Allied forces until it was safe to enter, which came after Victory in Europe, or V-E, day on May 8, 1945.

Major William Bronson, an engineering graduate of Stanford, was ordered to deliver one hundred V-2 rockets to a New Mexico test facility. His colleague, Major James Harper, a physics graduate of Fordham, was to identify and deliver the German experts who had developed and produced the V-2 rockets.

Major Bronson's performance was outstanding. Facing a deadline of June 1, 1945, the date the Soviets were due to occupy the Nordhausen area, the major had one hundred V-2 rockets, in whole or in parts, on railcars on their way to Antwerp to be loaded on freighters and then to New Mexico by way of Galveston, Texas.

Major Harper faced an even more difficult challenge. His superior Colonel Richards, as well as Richard's superiors, wanted the German rocket experts in New Mexico to direct the testing and, if it came to this, assist in launching the rockets against Japan. Colonel Richards had received approval to employ up to a hundred German "specialists" in the United States for a limited period, after which they were supposed to be sent home. Those chosen, ordered Allied Supreme Commander Dwight Eisenhower, can not have been ardent Nazis, members of the SS, or possible war criminals. Dr. Wernher von Braun, the technical director of the Nazi rocket program, along with those colleagues he selected, was "duly vetted" and packed off to the US.

Decades later it was revealed that the coveted rocket experts included ardent Nazis, commissioned officers of the SS, and alleged war criminals. Post World War II research established that "a sample of twenty-eight prominent [members of the von Braun team] shows that thirteen or fourteen had become [Nazi] party members and four, including von Braun, were in the SS" with the latter having been awarded the Knight's Cross, the Third Reich's highest decoration, personally by Adolf Hitler. (See *German Rocketeers in the Heart of Dixie: Making Sense of the Nazi*

Past During the Civil Rights Era by Monique Laney, Yale University Press, 2015.)

The US Army's Special Mission V-2 would prove to be a significant roadblock to Wilder's search for Hans Kammler. None knew Kammler better than Dornberger, von Braun, and key personnel involved in the design and production of V-2s. Yet none were made available to the prosecutor of the alleged Nordhausen war criminals. Kammler's colleagues testifying under oath would have been a banner event for Major Ben Wilder.

4

Hiding in Plain Sight

Continuing the exploits of Ben Wilder

YALE LAW SCHOOL GRADUATE AND SON of a German-American Jew, Ben Wilder had been recruited by the Office of Strategic Services (OSS) not only for his legal talent, but also for his being a Jew who spoke fluent German. His time with the OSS came to slightly over six months before his transfer to the newly created War Crimes Unit, a move that he sought as a connection to his search for Hans Kammler and to his appointment as the chief prosecutor of the alleged war criminals arrested at the Nordhausen rocket complex.

Ben's time in the OSS was more learning than doing: He was briefed on the history of the organization, what it was assigned to accomplish, and how it was organized to do what it had to do (whatever might be required to defeat the ene-my)—and it apparently had an unlimited budget to achieve its mission(s). By an executive order signed by President Franklin D. Roosevelt, the OSS director reported to the US Joint Chiefs of Staff chaired by Army General George C. Mar-shall. As Ben Wilder was to learn, however, the Joint Chiefs allowed the OSS to decide, in the interests of the [self-defined] national interest, for themselves what they could or could not do. As it turned out, there appeared to be no lim-it on their activities, and they had an unlimited budget to do it.

As Wilder was to discover later, when he encountered other Jews that shared his values, there were two wars to be fought. The first was against the Germans who had chosen to take on two powerful forces, the Soviet Union in the east and the British-American alliance in the west.

But there was another war being fought: a war against the German Nazis dedicated to annihi-lating all Jews, be they domestic or foreign. Play-ing a key role in this war against the Jews was SS General Hans Kammler, a man so unmoved

by suffering and dying that the French prisoners dubbed him Satan's Henchman. A dedicated
Nazi even before Adolf Hitler became German
chancellor, Kammler occupied the minor post
of Central SS Buildings Office early in the war.
By the final year of the war, however, he was the
third most powerful person in the SS hierarchy
topped only by Hitler and the SS Reichfürher
Heinrich Himmler.

In both private conversation with Wilder as well as sworn testimony, French prisoners brought up the following story involving
Kammler: A group of French prisoners sought
and gained a meeting with General Kammler
in which they pleaded for more humane treatment in exchange for their work. (In the underground rocket factory, deaths averaged 160 a
day.) Kammler heard them out, then responded
by nodding to his SS guards, who opened fire
on the delegation and killed eighty. Any hint of
sabotage, such as accidentally dropping a rocket
part, resulted in being executed by slowly being hanged from a crane. The bodies were left
dangling for several days. These mass executions
continued until the end of the war. All those involved, whether they be German workers or slave

laborers, understood how Obergruppenführer Hans Kammler wielded his power.

About three quarters from completion of a special program Major Wilder was assigned to, he was detached from the OSS and assigned to the War Crimes Unit to prepare to serve as chief prosecutor for the coming war crimes trials at the Dachau Concentration Camp, a follow-up to the Nuremberg trial of major war criminals. Wilder took the occasion to document what he knew (and didn't know) about General Hans Kammler.

Ben Wilder discovered early-on that productive sources for news of General Kammler were the Allied powers' T-Forces. As these units fell in place behind Allied combat forces, they were to seize and secure German military assets, be they persons, documents, or advanced weaponry. This included capturing and holding alleged Nazi war criminals.

As soon as it was known that Kammler, along with a select group of rocket experts, were at Oberammergau, a T-Force was alerted and the unit passed on that information to Major Wilder. But before he could act, Wilder was ordered to appear at OSS headquarters in London, a quite unusual order.

A private meeting with the OSS director was set and included two assignments: The first was that the director informed Wilder that he was about to offer the full resources of the OSS to US Supreme Court Justice Robert H. Jackson, who was designated to head the prosecution of major Nazi war criminals at Nuremberg. The OSS director wanted Wilder to join him at the trials because of his legal acumen, Jewish heritage, and fluency in German. With obvious delight, Major Ben Wilder accepted the assignment, but wondered if the head of the OSS's primary motivation was to seek a post-war mission, knowing that President Truman considered the OSS "out of control." (Truman abolished the agency by executive order in August 1946.)

Wilder's new assignment had to await the approval of Justice Jackson—who withdrew from his position of Associate Justice of the US Supreme Court to lead the prosecution. Meanwhile, another assignment requiring action was Project Safehaven.

Project Safehaven was established by the US State Department, which was fearful of the Nazi ideology being reborn in a safe haven supported by German officials' war treasures and plundering, such as the gold reserves seized by Germany from conquered nations. Project Safehaven was meant to locate and impede those efforts.

Several of the OSS's best counter-intelligence agents, Ben Wilder included, were being assigned to Project Safehaven. Led by a top state department official, the agents involved met in London for an extended briefing on the operation. It was here that Wilder got to know his fellow agents and speculated as to whom might assist him in his search for Hans Kammler.

The most interesting of Wilder's Safehaven agents was a dapper Hispanic with a remarkable and highly effective cover as the European representative of the Walt Disney Production Company of Hollywood, California. Europeans loved Walt Disney films, and this opened many doors to an American agent looking for Nazi loot and war criminals. This counterintelligence OSS agent covered the Iberian Peninsula, with Spain and Portugal having been designated as neutral in the war. In reality, the two nations were anything but, having supported the Third Reich both in spirit and military assets. As the peninsula was a prime target for the movement of Germany's stolen assets, Disney's European representative became the leader of Project Safehaven.

As Safehaven investigations established, there were many ways Nazi material wealth could be passed on to another country, especially to any one of the several that remained neutral. These included Sweden and Switzerland, as well as Spain and Portugal. But it was human assets, Germans with skills that other countries coveted, where "safe haven" was arranged with employment contracts. The lead employers for these assets, be they for the military or private companies, were in the United States. Previous service to the Third Reich presented no impediment. There was an ethical cost to this, Wilder realized, as the US ignored war crimes and chose not to render justice.

During this time, Wilder's attention was drawn to another OSS agent when he bragged about passing as an SS officer and retaining the uniform to someday thrill his grandchildren. Passing as an SS officer reminded the war crimes investigator of the report of a young SS officer leaving Oberammergau with SS Obergruppenführer Hans Kammler, who was reported killed in the fighting at Prague by either suicide or combat. He was declared officially deceased as of May 9, 1945, a decision that appeared to please most American security officials but not some OSS agents.

However, Obergruppenführer Hans Kammler, the third most powerful person in the Nazi hierarchy, may not have been killed on May 9, one day following the unconditional surrender of all German forces. It was widely rumored that he was badly wounded, requiring urgent medical treatment.

One leaked story had it that Otto Bergmann, a young junior SS officer, in a near-state of panic stuffed Kammler in the back of a sedan and headed west into territory occupied by American forces; he was determined to get Kammler into the nearest hospital and the bleeding stopped.

Within minutes of entering US-held territory, as this story went, the vehicle was surrounded by American troops. The Germans' coveted .32 Walther handguns were confiscated along with a machine pistol on the passenger seat besides Bergmann. Rushed to a hospital in a nearby city, the high-ranking SS officer, heavily guarded, received immediate and excellent treatment.

Within the hour, an Office of Strategic Services unit arrived and directed the GIs to return to their command without revealing who they had saved. By an OSS dictate, SS General Kammler would officially remain dead. Though a leading war criminal, to the OSS, Kammler was an important asset, one whom would remain hidden within the ranks of the OSS and later the CIA—in support, so it was claimed, of America's national interest.

Major Ben Wilder first accepted that Hans Kammler had been killed in Prague. When he learned that an aide to Kammler was in the custody of the OSS, however, he requested but was denied time to interrogate Bergmann. A break came when a former OSS agent revealed to Wilder his involvement in a plan to capture Kammler and use him as bait to land Reichminister Heinrich Himmler and deliver him to Nuremberg for trial.

Wilder accepted the plan as pure chutzpah. But giving it further thought, could it succeed? And if it somehow did, the Allies would have had a war criminal second only to Adolf Hitler in the dock at Nuremberg.

In his attempt to obtain confirmation from the CIA, Wilder faced a solid stone wall. The

CIA, especially its former OSS agents, wouldn't even admit they ever heard of an SS general named Kammler. The War Crimes Unit was now stuck with a possibly live, but reportedly dead, major Nazi war criminal.

No matter how persistent Major Ben Wilder was in pursuing someone he considered a major war criminal in the years following the war, whatever the CIA knew of Hans Kammler was covered by the veil of TOP SECRET. Before dropping his inquiry, however, Wilder learned two very significant items, one from Hermann Klaus, a state department officer he had encountered during his time on Project Safehaven who knew about secret Swiss bank accounts opened by Nazis, the other from a former OSS colleague, who mentioned that Kammler was seen with a pronounced limp. Wilder immediately connected the injured leg to reports he had heard describing the man who murdered Rudolf Baumann in Gallup, New Mexico.

A possible connection to the murder of Rudolf Baumann, Wilder concluded, had now been established. Until someone produced contrary evidence, Hans Kammler and Herman White were one and the same. And the murder of

Baumann, Ben Wilder further concluded, was tied to Kraus's revelation that the Third Reich had established a secret Swiss bank account.

The Swiss bank account had been arranged by Hitler's government to be used to purchase vital military assets. Kammler plus two other persons had access to the account. It seemed reasonable to believe that Rudolf Baumann, chief for rockets and advanced aircraft production, was one of the three, in as much as Kammler traveled often and could not be readily contacted. Eventually, Wilder came around to a logical third person who might have access to the account: Kammler's superior, Reichminister Heinrich Himmler! He, too, must have had a postwar life in mind. In fact, one unverified report stated that Himmler had requested of Kammler that he, Himmler, be provided with an experimental long-range aircraft. Kammler ignored the request.

Ben Wilder's contact in the US State Department, Hermann Klaus, was as determined as Wilder to track down leading Nazi war criminals. And he was a valuable source for information, in this instance, cash stashed in a numbered Swiss bank account. Nazis with personal Swiss bank accounts would have little or no difficulty converting art, real estate, or gold to cash. Also applicable to the Kammler story, a numbered account would require the multiple holders' approval to close the account. No account holder could assign his right to any outsider, except as a provision in his will, noted a Swiss banker.

Wilder and Klaus agreed that the holders of the numbered Swiss account were Himmler, Kammler, and V2 production manager Baumann. With Himmler's suicide, this left Kammler and Baumann to tap into the account. This explained to Wilder's satisfaction that Kammler's visit to the US was to obtain Baumann's approval to close the account and share the money. Baumann balked, however, probably out of fear it would reveal him as a war criminal. The death of Baumann would then leave Kammler as the sole Swiss account holder. But would it? Overlooked, it seems, was the reality that Kammler was officially declared killed in the battle at Prague. If he came forward and declared himself to be Hans Kammler, he would be exposed as a war criminal. His new identity, provided by his OSS and CIA protectors, came at great expense!

Word spread throughout the intelligence services that the so-called Cold War had all but ended the search for Nazi war criminals. Remaining active, however, were Jews—both domestic and foreign, especially in Israel—who had dug the Tunnels of Hell. In France, with its large community of survivors of the underground factory, much speculation emerged as to the new identity of Satan's Henchman and where the OSS (or its successor, the Central Intelligence Agency) might have placed him in a safe haven, as had been arranged for other Nazi war criminals brought to the United States as military assets. In the case of Hans Kammler, the record was purged of whole families being selected as slave labor at the V-2 rocket factory, with the very old and very young separated and, as an SS officer expressed it, "put out of their misery." Hitler's production czar wanted no unproductive labor.

The most commonly held belief of the fate of Hans Kammler is that he was provided a new identity and a one-way ticket to Argentina. As this had been accomplished for other known Nazi war criminals, it followed as an accepted practice during the Cold War. Too obvious, Ben Wilder reasoned, and he discounted that possibility. He pointed out to colleagues, who wanted to load the Kammler indictment of multiple war crimes, that he could be hung but once so get it done and move on.

Ben Wilder had returned to his position in the Justice Department after having failed in his effort to locate Kammler "dead or alive." Not long after, he received a note from one of his fellow OSS agents asking if he could come see him about a very private matter. The ex-agent, he learned, was very ill and a patient at the nearby veterans hospital.

What the ex-OSS agent had to offer was a bombshell revelation: Kammler had been in the hands of the OSS and, later, the CIA following the termination of the OSS in August 1946. Badly wounded at Prague, his aide had stumbled into an American unit while seeking medical treatment. The unit promptly contacted the OSS, who took it from there. Once recovered from his damaged leg, he was provided a new identity and soon became a trusted American counterintelligence agent. This was not an uncommon practice as the Cold War heated up. In Wilder's attempt, however, to learn Kammler's new identity and location, he once again discovered the CIA "never heard of Kammler."

In frustration, the war crimes investigator had closed the book on Kammler when he received an unexpected call from John Wilson, who described himself as the director of security at the state department. Hermann Kraus, Wilder's friend and contact at State, had urged Wilson to call Wilder and relate an interesting occurrence connected to Kammler.

As Wilson described it, he had arrived at his office that morning and discovered a file on his desk he had not requested. It was the personnel file of one Jacob Hoffmann, a State employee, currently the cultural attache at the American embassy in Chile. It was the security investigative report on Hoffmann that drew Ben Wilder's rapt attention.

According to the report, Jacob Hoffmann, a German Jew, had read *Mein Kampf* even before Hitler came to power and realized what was to come. Though his parents refused to leave their beloved Germany, Jacob immigrated, first to Czechoslovakia, then in 1938 to Italy, where he was sheltered in convents during the war, after which he obtained employment, first with the American army, later with the US State Department. But it was his personal description that fired-up Ben Wilder: same age as Kammler, a gimpy left leg, well educated, spoke fluent German, and not very attractive.

By the end of the day, Ben Wilder had applied for a visa to Chile, arranged air travel to its capital Santiago, and assumed the role of a freelance magazine writer interested in the early Germans who had immigrated to Chile. (From his research, Wilder knew of Colonia Dignidad, an isolated Chilean community of ex-Nazis.)

Upon arriving at the American embassy, Wilder asked for an interview with the cultural attaché, only to learn that he had died from an accidental fall while jogging on a hiking trail high above the city. Case closed, declared the Chilean police department. The next call was to John Wilson, security chief of the State Department, who immediately had Wilder meeting with the embassy's security official.

"Chilean authorities are too quick to close an investigation," offered Jason Sender. "Our investigation is open, and we have a witness, one of our embassy staff."

While jogging behind, the embassy employee saw two men on the trail talking, and as he jogged around them, he recognized Jacob Hoffmann but not the second man. Some thirty feet beyond the two men, he encounter a rock that had fallen on the trail, which he proceeded to toss into the valley. It was then, as he glanced back, he saw Hoffmann falling backward, and as he did, he grabbed the other person with both tumbling into the valley. A sad accident, declared the Santiago police. Case closed.

Yes, case close, mused Ben Wilder. As he was flying back to Washington—and to his position at the justice department, he wondered if Hoffmann, perhaps suspecting that he was about to be exposed as a war criminal, might have committed suicide and taken the second person with him. Perhaps, or perhaps truly an accident. But now, this was part of his past, not his future.

A month later, however, came a call from the security chief at State. "Just thought you'd like to know, we were able to open Hoffmann's large safe deposit box, and lo and behold, there were six bars of gold! How about coming aboard and solving this rather strange matter," White offered with a smile.

"Sorry, friend," Wilder replied. "You're on your own. For me, Hoffmann-Kammler is in my past, and that is where it shall remain forever! Goodbye, good hunting, and may the looted gold find its rightful owner!"

Author's Note

AT THE END OF 1944, I WAS ASSIGNED TO the 404th Fighter Group, 506th Fighter Squad-ron, as a replace-ment fighter-bomb-er pilot. During the final months of the European conflict, I completed thirty-six combat sorties, in-cluded one having a possible bearing on the ultimate fate of Hans Kammler.

My final combat sortie came in early May 1945 when my flight was directed to surveil the highway

Robert Huddleston serving as a young fighter pilot in November 1944.

leading south out of Prague, Czechoslovakia. The Russians began their offensive in the final battle of the war. The 506th Fighter Squadron mission was to prevent the Germans from bringing up reserve forces. In fact, traffic on the highway headed west consisted of Germans, especially SS units, seeking to escape capture by the Russians. My combat report included "one large vehicle destroyed." Could that vehicle have included SS General Hans Kammler? Perhaps.

Readers and critics may wonder about *Satan's Henchman* being autobiographical... *Autobiographical* simply means that the published work deals with the writer's own life. And since nonfiction elements are vital to this story, I have designated it a *semi-autobiographical* novel.

Robert Huddleston was awarded the coveted silver wings of an Army Air Corps pilot at the age of nineteen. This was followed by extensive training in the P-47 Thunderbolt, the aircraft he would pilot in combat against German military forces in the air or on the ground.

After the war, a university education under the GI Bill was followed by employment at New Mexico's White Sands Missile Range, where German rocket experts were employed. He then moved onto Washington, DC, joining the newly established space agency NASA, first at the Goddard Space Flight Center in nearby Maryland, later at NASA headquarters. Huddleston has degrees from the University of Missouri and George Washington University, and he graduated from the Defense University in Washington, DC, as a representative of NASA.

Departing federal service, he became a

freelance writer publishing articles, essays, book reviews, and short stories. He has also published a biography of a Mexican-American patriot, *Edmundo: From Chiapas, Mexico, to Park Avenue* (2007); the novella *An American Pilot with the Luftwaffe* (2014); and the novel *Love and War: A Father and Son in Two World Wars* (2020). He now resides in a retirement community in Chapel Hill, North Carolina.